# Single-Celled Organisms

Elaine Pascoe

Photographs by Dwight Kuhn

2/04        15.25

Published in 2003 by The Rosen Publishing Group, Inc.
29 East 21st Street, New York, NY 10010

First Edition

Editor: Natashya Wilson
Book Design: Emily Muschinske
Layout Design: Eric DePalo

Photo Credits: All photographs © Dwight Kuhn.

Pascoe, Elaine.
Single-celled organisms / Elaine Pascoe.— 1st ed.
    p. cm. — (A kid's guide to the classification of living things)
Includes bibliographical references (p.    ).
  ISBN 0-8239-6312-8 (lib. bdg.)
1. Prokaryotes—Juvenile literature. 2. Microorganisms—Juvenile literature. [1. Prokaryotes. 2. Microorganisms.]
I. Title.
  QR74.5 .P374 2003
  579—dc21
                                                              2001006645

Manufactured in the United States of America

# Contents

# Classifying Living Things

Right now thousands of tiny living things are all around you. They are close enough to touch, but they are too small to see. They are single-celled **organisms**.

Scientists use a system called classification to keep track of living things. Classification is a way of creating order by putting things in groups. In a supermarket, cereals are in one aisle and soups are in another. In the same way, scientists sort living things based on the ways in which they are alike.

Most scientists sort living things into five **kingdoms**. Each kingdom is sorted into smaller groups until a group contains only one type, or **species**, of organism. The monera and protist kingdoms are made up almost entirely of single-celled organisms.

*This diagram shows how the monera and protist kingdoms can be sorted into groups. The protist kingdom has been sorted into even smaller groups.*

**Fungus Kingdom**

**Animal Kingdom**

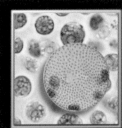

**Protist Kingdom**

**Monera Kingdom**

**Plant Kingdom**

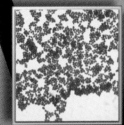

**Bacteria**

**Cyanobacteria**

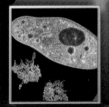

**Protozoa**

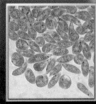

**Euglena**

**Algae**

**Slime Molds and Water Molds**

**Amoeba**

**Paramecium**

**Chamydomonas**

**Volvox**

5

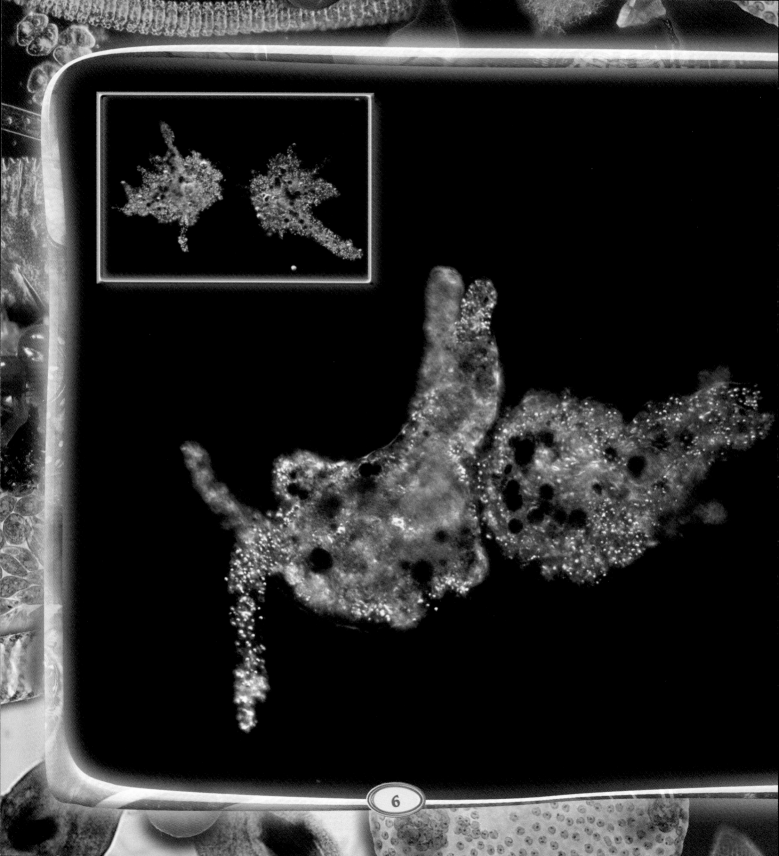

# Just One Cell

Cells are tiny units that make up all living things. Your body has millions of cells, all working together. A single-celled organism has only one cell.

The single-celled organisms known as bacteria and blue-green algae make up the monera kingdom. Monerans are the simplest of all living things. Most living cells have a structure called a **nucleus.** The nucleus holds the cell's **genes** and controls how the cell works. A moneran is so simple that it has no true nucleus. Most monerans **reproduce** by dividing. One cell splits into two cells. They go their separate ways.

Other single-celled organisms belong to the protist kingdom. Protists have true nuclei. They are more advanced than monerans, but they are still very simple.

*An amoeba is a type of protist. This amoeba is reproducing by dividing itself in two. Inset: When division is complete, there are two amoebas.*

# Bacteria: Simplest of All

Bacteria belong to the monera kingdom. They are the simplest of all single-celled organisms. Most bacteria can only be seen with a microscope. The most common kinds of bacteria look like balls, rods, or coiled springs.

Even though you can't see them, bacteria are everywhere. There are bacteria in the soil, in the air, and in the water. They are even inside your body! Bacteria do not produce their own food. Many bacteria feed on wastes or on dead plants and animals. As many as 100 million cells of bacteria may live in one drop of spoiled milk. Some bacteria feed on living plants and animals. Many of these bacteria cause sicknesses.

*Most bacteria are so small that they can be seen only through a microscope. These are ball-shaped bacteria.*

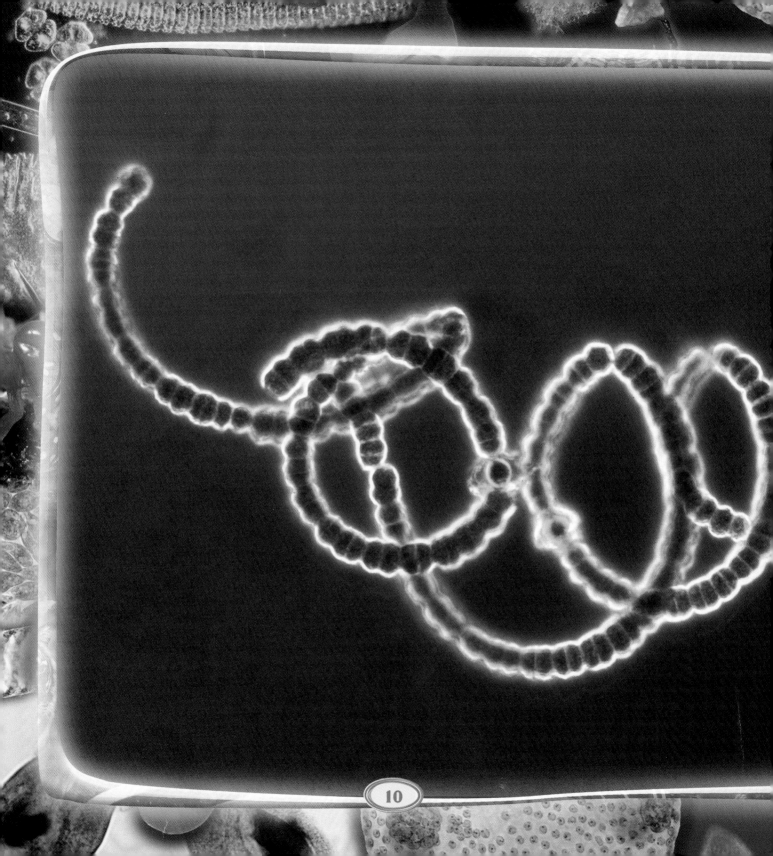

# Cyanobacteria: Blue-Green Algae

The monerans known as blue-green algae are not true algae. They are not all blue-green, either. Scientists also call these living things **cyanobacteria**.

Like bacteria, blue-green algae have no true nuclei. Unlike bacteria, they produce their own food. Blue-green algae contain materials called **pigments**. These pigments take energy from sunlight and use it to make food. Pigments also give blue-green algae their colors.

Blue-green algae live in water and in damp soil. Some kinds clump together to form slimy strings, balls, or sheets. Some kinds link together to form long chains. Some kinds of blue-green algae do not clump together. A kind of scum that floats on ponds in the summer is made up of blue-green algae.

 *Blue-green algae got their name because they look like true algae, and because many types are blue or green.*

Blue-green algae can often be found floating in water. Seen through a microscope, this mass of blue-green algae looks like a clump of green peas.

Some types of blue-green algae clump together to form long, thin strands.

The most common types of bacteria are shaped like balls, rods, or spirals. This picture shows bacteria of all three shapes.

These bacteria (above) live in people's mouths. They form a layer on the teeth called plaque. Brushing the teeth helps to keep the bacteria from making cavities.

# Protozoa: On the Move

Protozoans are single-celled organisms that belong to the protist kingdom. Like all protists, protozoans have true nuclei and other structures inside of their cells.

If you look at a drop of pond water through a microscope, you will see protozoans wiggling around. Most protozoans live in water or in soil. They move to find food. Some protozoans move by waving the special hairs, called **cilia**, on their bodies. Some move by wagging their tail-like **flagella**. Some protozoans, such as **amoebas**, ooze along with their entire bodies.

Protozoans feed mostly on bits of plant and animal material or on other tiny organisms. Some protozoans are **parasites** that live inside plants or animals.

*This protozoan moves with the help of the tiny, hairlike cilia on its body.*

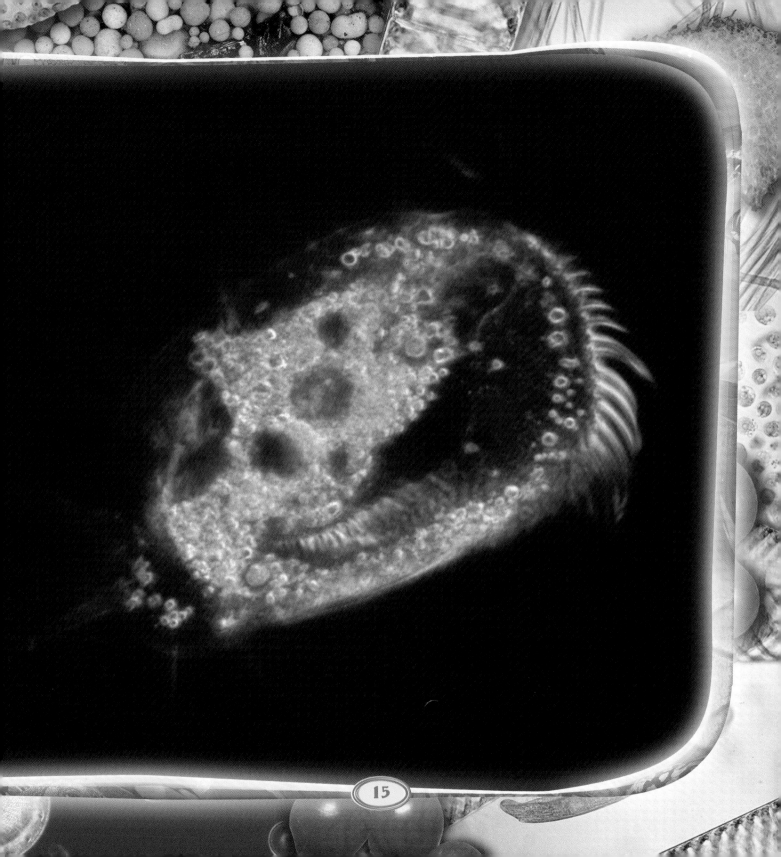

You would need a microscope to see this tiny protozoan. It is swimming among strands of green algae.

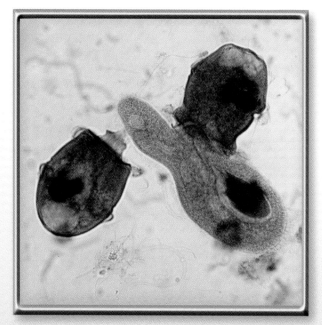

Some protozoans eat other protozoans. Here a protozoan called a paramecium is being attacked by two other protozoans, called didinium.

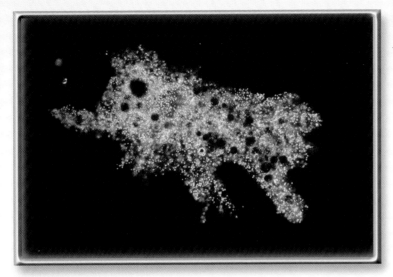

*An amoeba has no regular shape. It moves by flowing its body in the direction in which it wants to go.*

*A paramecium is shaped like a slipper. The large, dark oval in the middle of this paramecium's body is its nucleus.*

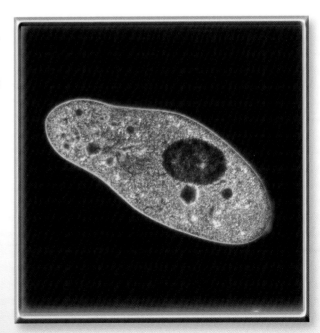

# Euglena: Best of Two Worlds

Euglena also belong to the protist kingdom. A euglena is like a plant in some ways and like an animal in other ways. It can make its own food the way a plant can. It can move around as an animal can. Some scientists put euglena and their relatives in the same group as algae.

Euglena and their relatives live mainly in freshwater. As do protozoans, they move around in the water. They also have a pigment called **chlorophyll**. Chlorophyll allows them to use the energy in sunlight to make food. It gives euglena their greenish color.

Euglena also have an unusual feature called an eyespot. It is not a true eye, but it reacts to light. It helps the tiny creatures to find sunlight.

*You can tell euglena from protozoans by euglena's green color and eyespots. Here the eyespots look like fuzzy, reddish dots.*

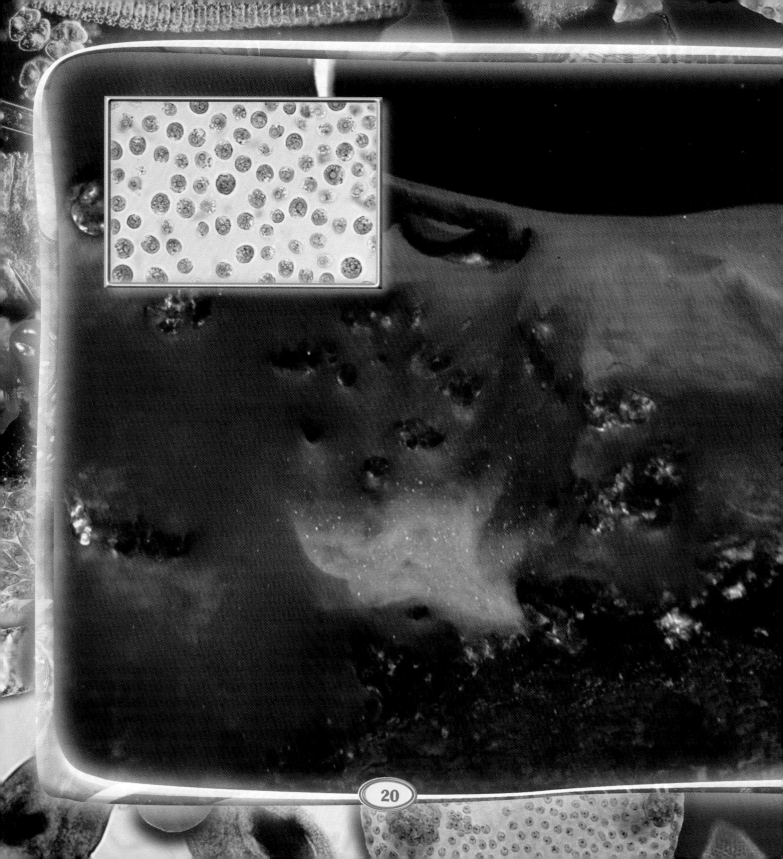

# Algae: Producers

Algae are protists that make their own food, as do plants. They are much simpler than plants, though. They don't have roots, stems, or leaves. They also differ from plants in other ways, which is why scientists place them with the protists.

Algae live in freshwater and in salt water. Scientists sort them by their colors. Pigments give algae color and allow them to use the Sun's energy to make food.

Golden algae and certain kinds of green algae are single-celled organisms. Some green algae gather in bunches made of many individuals. Other types of algae are **multicelled** organisms. They include seaweeds that are members of the red algae and the brown algae groups.

*Red algae are multicelled organisms. Inset: This type of green algae, chamydomonas, is a single-celled organism.*

Some types of algae, such as these volvox algae, gather together into bunches called colonies.

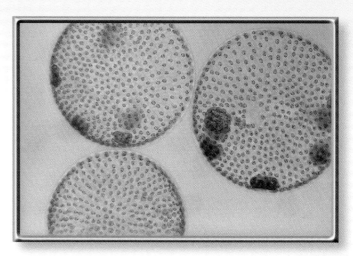

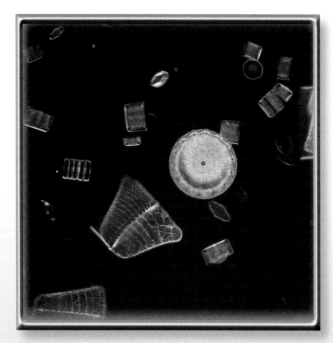

Diatoms are golden algae found in the ocean. With their glasslike walls, they are sometimes called the jewels of the sea.

Algae grow well in small, still lakes such as this one. The growth of algae is called an algae bloom.

Rockweed is a multicelled type of algae. This rockweed grew in Maine.

Green algae comes in different shapes. These are different types of green algae.

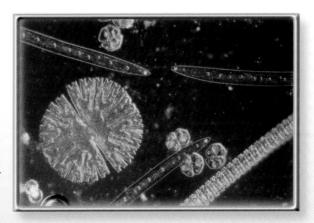

# Slime Molds and Water Molds: Decomposers

Slime molds and water molds are protists that live in damp places. They play an important role in nature. They help to **decompose**, or break down, dead plants and animals. Slime molds and water molds are not true molds. Slime molds can move. True molds cannot. Water molds reproduce in a different way than true molds do, and they live in water and soil.

A slime mold has two life stages. In its feeding stage, it looks like a splatter of jelly. It moves very slowly, feeding on rotting logs and leaves. In the next stage, the slime mold reproduces. It sprouts fuzzy spines called fruiting bodies. The fruiting bodies give off **spores**. The wind carries away the spores. If they land in damp places, new slime molds will grow.

*Water mold grows on the body of a black fly larva. Inset: These are the fuzzy fruiting bodies of a slime mold.*

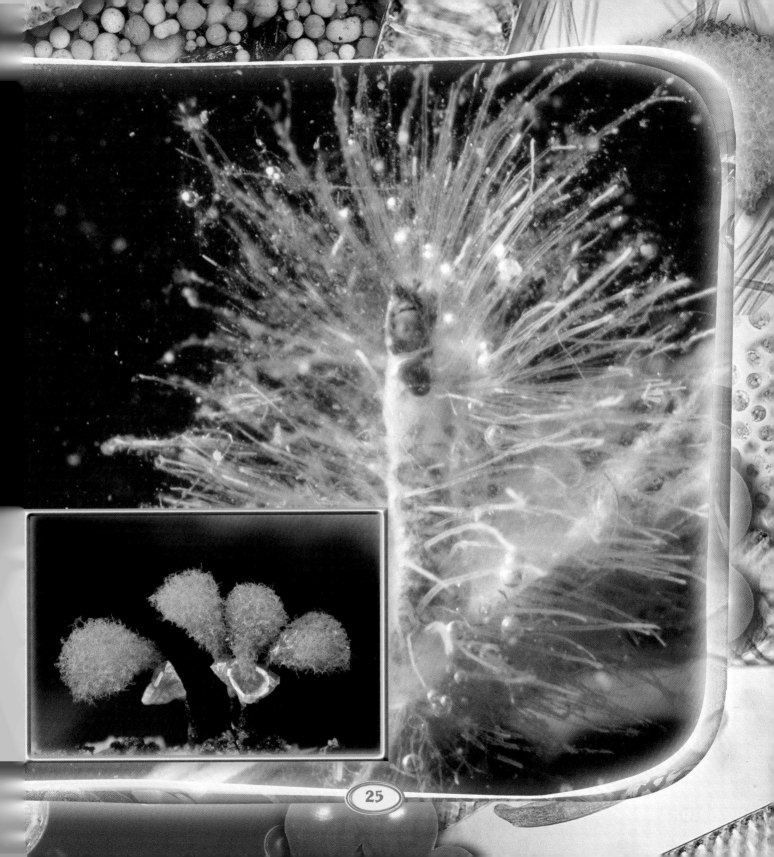

# Harmful and Helpful

Some single-celled organisms cause a great deal of harm. Bacteria spoil food. Bacteria and protozoans cause many sicknesses. A few kinds of algae are poisonous.

Single-celled organisms also play helpful roles. These simple living things are food for many animals. They help to clean up wastes and dead plants and animals.

Certain bacteria in soil help plants to grow. They add **nitrogen** to the soil. Plants need nitrogen to grow. Other bacteria help people and other animals to digest their food. Some of these bacteria live right inside of your intestines!

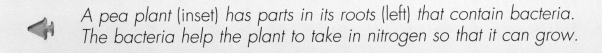

*A pea plant (inset) has parts in its roots (left) that contain bacteria. The bacteria help the plant to take in nitrogen so that it can grow.*

This slime mold is in its feeding stage. It is moving along a rotting log.

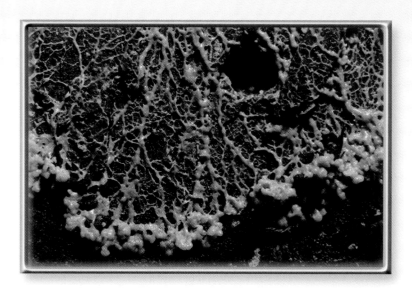

This is what the fruiting bodies of a slime mold look like when they first sprout. They will soon become fuzzy as they produce spores.

Protozoans live in this termite's intestines. The protozoans help the termite to break down the wood it eats.

This water mold is helping to break down the body of a dead fish.

# Living and Nonliving

Some living things are huge. Others are so small that you need a microscope to see them, but all living things have some traits in common.

All living things can reproduce. Cats have kittens. Bacteria divide to make more bacteria. All living things use food, too. Plants and some single-celled organisms make their own food. Other living things get their food in different ways. All living things react to the world around them. Nonliving things do none of those things. Your bicycle will never reproduce, grow, or use food. It will not know if you ride it. In these ways, nonliving things differ from living things.

*Rocks are nonliving things. They never need food. They don't know if they are wet or dry.*

# Glossary

**amoebas** (uh-MEE-buhz) Protozoans that move around by oozing their bodies in the direction in which they want to go.

**chlorophyll** (KLOR-uh-fil) Green pigment inside living things that allows them to use energy from sunlight to make their own food.

**cilia** (SIH-lee-uh) Hairlike structures that some living things use to move.

**cyanobacteria** (sy-uh-noh-bak-TEER-ee-uh) Another name for blue-green algae.

**decompose** (dee-kum-POHZ) To break down the cells of dead things.

**flagella** (fluh-JEH-luh) Tail-like structures that some living things use to move.

**genes** (JEENZ) Materials inside cells that controls the traits of living things.

**kingdoms** (KEENG-duhmz) The first level of groups into which scientists sort living things.

**multicelled** (mul-tee-SELD) Made up of many cells.

**nitrogen** (NY-troh-jen) A substance that living things need to grow.

**nucleus** (NOO-clee-uhs) A structure inside a cell that holds the cell's genes and that controls how the cell works. The plural is nuclei (NOO-klee-eye).

**organisms** (OR-geh-nih-zuhmz) Living things.

**parasites** (PAR-uh-syts) Living things that live in and feed on other living things.

**pigments** (PIG-mehntz) Materials that color cells and that have a variety of roles inside cells.

**reproduce** (ree-pruh-DOOS) To have babies.

**species** (SPEE-sheez) The smallest grouping in the classification of living things.

**spores** (SPORZ) Special cells that can grow into new living things.

# Index

# Web Sites

Due to the changing nature of Internet links, PowerKids Press has developed an online list of Web sites related to the subject of this book. This site is updated regularly. Please use this link to access the list:

www.powerkidslinks.com/kgclt/sinclorg/

## DATE DUE

| DATE DUE | |
|---|---|
| NOV 1 5 2004 | |
| | |
| | |
| | |
| | |
| | |
| | |
| | |
| | |
| | |
| | |
| | |
| | |
| | |
| | |
| | |
| | |

GAYLORD                                    PRINTED IN U.S.A.